CAN GOD BLESS AMERICA?

The Biblical Pathway to Blessing

JOHN MACARTHUR

W PUBLISHING GROUP™

www.wpublishinggroup.com

A Division of Thomas Nelson, Inc.
www.ThomasNelson.com

CAN GOD BLESS AMERICA?

Copyright © 2002 by John MacArthur.
Published by The W Publishing Group,
a unit of Thomas Nelson Publishers,
P. O. Box 141000, Nashville, TN 37214.

All scripture quotations in this book, except those noted
otherwise, are from the New King James Version, © 1984 by
Thomas Nelson, Inc.

Quotations marked NASB are from the New American
Standard Bible,
© 1960, 1962, 1963, 1968, 1971, 1972, 1973, 1975,
1977, 1988, and 1995 by The Lockman Foundation,
and are used by permission.

Quotations marked KJV are from the
King James Version of the Bible.

ISBN 0-8499-555-99

Printed in the United States of America
02 03 04 05 PHX 5 4 3 2

CONTENTS

INTRODUCTION

*I*n this era of war against terrorism, a sudden wave of patriotism has revived the slogan "God Bless America." The sentiment is expressed everywhere. It is even seen, ironically, on bumper-stickers adjacent to other bumper-stickers expressing humanistic and atheistic sentiments. One assumes that even those who don't believe in God want His blessing on our nation.

Anti-God philosophies and anti-Christian world-views now clearly dominate most of modern Western society. God has systematically been removed from public discourse; prayer has been virtually banned from the public arena; agnosticism and humanism dominate public policy. So it is remarkable that the slogan "God Bless America" has seen such a widespread revival. We have to wonder what most people have in mind when they repeat the slogan.

Many believe this nation's devotion to freedom, equality, charity, justice, and individual rights has led God to bless us with riches and comfort. But as America has become more humanistic, it has also become more prosperous. Now more affluent than ever, we are also more atheistic than ever. While people reject the God of Scripture as their Sovereign, they still claim Him as their servant. For some people that is *all* they mean by "God Bless America."

Originally, "God Bless America" was a *prayer* for divine blessing. In its current form it sometimes seems nothing more than a patriotic battle-cry—usually intoned without much serious reflection. Perhaps it is sometimes recited like a mantra—as if merely invoking God's name could garner His blessing.

Some apparently believe that America enjoys God's blessing by divine right. After all, God *has* blessed America throughout history to a remarkable degree. But His blessings are not measured—as most people believe—by material affluence, power, and world dominance. The greatest blessings God has graciously given America have been *spiritual* blessings—knowledge of the good news of salvation in Christ, freedom for the gospel to be propagated, sweeping revivals like those of the Great Awakenings, and growth and spiritual prosperity for the church in our nation. The sad truth is that all those blessings have been in serious jeopardy since long before the terrorist strikes reminded us that our freedom and material prosperity hang by a fragile thread.

What do we really mean when we invoke God's blessing on our nation? Do people in America truly long for the spiritual awakening that would be the necessary condition for true divine blessing, or would the policy-makers and media moguls in our society be as hostile to such a revival as they are to the threat of terrorism? Are people in America prepared to embrace God's Son as Lord and Savior, or do they just want God's favor on their own terms?

And what are the means by which the people of God should seek to have God's blessing on our nation? Can we help position modern society to receive God's blessing merely by influencing public policy through politics and protest, or is something more needed to fulfill the conditions under which God will bless our nation? Can external moral reform alone make America fit for God's blessing, or is something even deeper needed in the lives of most Americans?

To ask such questions is to answer them. Scripture is clear that a wholesale spiritual renewal, brought about through the clear and persuasive preaching of the gospel of Jesus Christ, is the sole pathway to divine blessing. What is needed is not merely moral reform, but spiritual regeneration. And unless this occurs on a widespread scale that deeply impacts all of society, we will continue to forfeit the true blessings of God for our nation. Merely reciting the slogan "God Bless America" will do nothing for us, until it becomes a heartfelt prayer for spiritual renewal and regeneration through the gospel.

The remedy to our nation's moral and spiritual woes must begin at the house of God. The process starts with personal repentance. And if Christians truly want to see God's blessing on our society, *we* ought to be models of genuine contrition and humility, rather than merely pointing fingers of blame at the evils of secular society. God Himself said to Israel, "If My *people who are called by My name* will humble themselves, and pray and seek My face, and turn from their wicked ways, then I will hear from heaven, and will forgive their sin and heal their land" (2 Chronicles 7:14, emphasis added).

Christians concerned about the moral evils of society often opt for the wrong remedies, as if all that were needed to cure the spiritual malaise of our nation were some kind of federal legislation against abortion, sexual promiscuity, pornography and other forms of corruption.

Political remedies to our nation's moral ills are no cure for the underlying spiritual problems. Of all people, Christians ought to know that, and the preponderance of our efforts ought to be focused on proclaiming the truth that can genuinely set people free.

Lives, not just laws, need to be transformed before America will be in a position to ask for and expect God's blessing. The blessings of God cannot be acquired by any legislative process. Law cannot make people righteous. Scripture is clear on this. "If right-eousness comes through the law, then Christ died in vain" (Galatians 2:21). No one is justified by works of law, but by faith in Jesus Christ (Galatians 2:16). And saving faith is an individual matter; it cannot be imposed by legislative force.

In other words, society as a whole cannot be deliv-ered from moral bankruptcy unless individual lives are redeemed and transformed by the power of Christ. If that conviction does not frame the priorities of the people of God and drive the activities of the church on earth, asking God to bless America is a waste of time.

God has revealed in the Bible there are several clear conditions under which a nation can expect God's blessing. My desire in this little book is to examine those conditions and to challenge the people of God to lead the way in pursuing God's blessing for ourselves and for our nation.

I

THE QUESTION NO ONE IS ASKING

"Draw near to God and He will draw near to you.
Cleanse your hands, you sinners; and purify your hearts, you
double-minded. Lament and mourn and weep! Let your laughter
be turned to mourning and your joy to gloom. Humble yourselves
in the sight of the Lord, and He will lift you up."
—JAMES 4: 8–10

One of the more hopeful features of our nation's response to the terrorist attacks of September 11, 2001, was an immediate heightening of interest in spiritual things. Church attendance rose dramatically, at least for a few weeks. People talked openly of God and wondered aloud if the attacks on Washington and New York held any spiritual or prophetic significance. Was God angry with America? Why did He permit such a horrific catastrophe? Was there a spiritual message in all of this? What did it mean?

Such concerns have changed the tone of the national conversation. Life in America has suddenly taken on a more serious and sober mien. People's thoughts have turned naturally to weightier matters. Multitudes are now approaching life less superficially and less frivolously. And it is probably thanks to that mood-change, combined with the patriotic fervor that has swept the nation since the attacks, that the familiar slogan "God Bless America" has been brought out of mothballs and has become a national rallying-cry.

That slogan, and the music associated with it, date back to 1918, when composer Irving Berlin (an immigrant from Siberia) penned the song as part of a musical review during the difficult days of American involvement in World War I. The song received little notice at the time, but Irving Berlin revised and re-released it in 1938 when a new war was threatening Europe. He said he conceived the revised edition of the song as a plea for peace in an era when most Americans were hoping to avert American involvement in another foreign war.

But the song retained its popularity even after America was drawn into World War II. In the minds of most Americans, "God Bless America" became a plea that God would bless the American war effort with success. And thus the song's opening line quickly became fixed in the American psyche as both a prayer and a patriotic slogan.

Today, in the wake of the new war on terrorism, "God Bless America" has once again become something of a national anthem. It is still a fitting prayer, and for many, I am sure, it is a heartfelt prayer. It would be a mistake to dismiss its popularity as nothing more than shallow sentimentality. These are dark and difficult times, and most Americans deeply sense the need for God's blessing.

To a large degree, I suppose, the American people's yearning for God's blessing is prompted by a desire for His immediate protection. For many, "Bless America" means, simply, "Preserve our nation." For others, it means something as down-to-earth as, "God, don't let me die. Don't let my children die. Don't let my spouse die." For still others, it might mean something more mundane: "Don't let the stock market drop any further"; or, "Stop the rise in unemployment." In many mouths it is a prayer for the preservation of our nation's freedom and prosperity.

"Blessing," then, is associated with protection, safety, freedom, and prosperity. In that sense, the slogan perfectly resonates with the current mood of the nation.

In fact, it expresses popular sentiment so well that even the usually-vocal atheists and militant agnostics have, for the most part, disappeared into the shadows. Early on, there were a couple of failed attempts by the American Civil Liberties Union to have "God Bless America" removed from school bulletin-boards and public marquees. But that effort proved so unpopular that it was quickly dropped in order to avoid an angry backlash. God's name is back in public discourse, if only for the sake of this slogan.

In some of the early ceremonies commemorating

those who died in the terrorist attacks, "God Bless America" was incongruously sung alongside John Lennon's song "Imagine." Lennon's lyrics wistfully long for a world without religion, without the hope of heaven and without the threat of hell, where people live only for today. "Imagine" pleads for the day when everyone will embrace such a vacuous worldview. John Lennon apparently imagined that nothing would matter to anyone in a world like that, and therefore people would finally be able to live in perfect harmony. The sentiments expressed in Lennon's song are practically the polar opposite of those expressed in Irving Berlin's.

Thankfully, "God Bless America," rather than "Imagine," is the song and the slogan that has emerged as the rallying-cry of the American people. The average American cannot imagine a world in which there is no God, no religion, and no heaven—where nothing really matters. If that were indeed the case, the terrorist acts would not have stirred our passions in the first place.

The vast majority of Americans know in their souls

and their consciences that God *does* exist and His blessing is essential to the future peace of their lives and nation. Unfortunately, most Americans are without God and therefore without any palpable hope. They affirm the slogan but are ignorant of the God to whom it is addressed (cf. Acts 17:22–31).

Most Americans are, to one degree or another, in a state of fear. They are crying out to heaven for an invisible means of support from an invisible God against an invisible enemy. They *hope* God is omnipresent, omniscient, and omnipotent. They hope He is interested in their plight. But even more urgently, they hope He will have mercy on our nation. That is why the cry "God Bless America" is so prevalent and so often laden with deep emotion.

Will God bless America? *Can* God bless America? *Should* God bless America? Or is our society on the brink of judgment rather than blessing? Are the recent catastrophes merely harbingers of something worse yet to come?

Given the moral bankruptcy of modern society, it seems fair to ask such questions. Are we fit for blessing, or has our nation forfeited any claim to divine blessing? If God *did* bless America, what would He be saying about His holiness? What would He be saying about our morality? What would He be saying about our spiritual condition?

Can God bless America without compromising His reputation as a holy God? That is the vital question.

Of course, God can always do whatever He wants, whenever He wants. But when it comes to blessing, He has clearly and repeatedly set down conditions.

Listen carefully to the song, "God Bless America," and you will see that there is no verse that identifies the conditions for divine blessing. Nor do Americans seem to be opening their Bibles to try to find out what the conditions are. I don't hear anyone asking, "God, what do *we* need to do to be blessed?"

In fact, to raise that question might be seen by many as a serious intrusion. Do the American people really want to know the conditions that precede God's blessing? The sentiment sometimes seems to be, "Don't tell us what to do; just bless us," as if God were not supposed to ask anything of *us*. Many would prefer blessing without any conditions being imposed. Give us protection. Give us safety. Give us freedom. Give us prosperity. Just don't meddle with our morality.

We rarely hear anyone today calling people to repentance. In many quarters, it is considered bad protocol and bad form to remind people that the Word of God makes demands on us. The reproofs, rebukes, and exhortations of God's Word are simply not what most people today want to hear. They won't tolerate it (cf. 2 Timothy 4:3). Therefore even some preachers avoid mentioning such matters. Sadly, when sin is not confronted, sinners do not perceive their need for grace and forgiveness.

Frankly, our nation is in no position at the moment to be blessed. We're actually more likely to be cursed by God.

So is our prayer for blessing futile? I don't believe it is futile. But we need to understand that a prayer for divine blessing presupposes a willingness to cultivate the conditions under which divine blessing can come.

What are those conditions? Let's turn to Scripture and investigate the question almost no one is asking.

James 4:7–10 gives a list of ten commands that set forth the conditions for divine blessing. James addresses his epistle to Christian people (he frequently refers to them as "my brethren"), so some commentators have assumed that these ten imperatives apply only to believers, rather than to unbelievers who have never been born again.

But that misses the point. *This* list of directives is addressed to "sinners" and the "double-minded" (v. 8), and those are terms that are normally used in Scripture to describe unredeemed people. James is evidently concerned that some in his audience are not truly redeemed. He calls them "Adulterers and adulteresses!" (v. 4), and he warns them that friendship with the world is enmity with God. Apparently he believed some of these people, though professing to be believers, had never been truly born again. And so he outlines for them what true repentance demands of them: "Submit to God. Resist the devil and he will flee from you. Draw near to God and He will draw near to you. Cleanse your hands, you sinners; and purify your hearts, you double-minded. Lament and mourn and weep! Let your laughter be turned to mourning and your joy to gloom. Humble yourselves in the sight of the Lord, and He will lift you up" (vv. 7–10).

Submit to God

The first of the ten commands is "submit." James uses a Greek term that has military overtones. It speaks of compliance with the will of someone at a higher rank. He employs a passive form, indicating that our submission to God must be voluntary.

Luke uses the same word when he speaks of Jesus'

boyhood submission to His parents (Luke 2:51). Paul uses it of the believer's duty to submit to governmental authority (Romans 13:1). So it carries the connotation of acquiescence and voluntary compliance to an authority one is obligated to submit to in the first place.

Our duty to God begins with a recognition of His right to rule over us. Therefore, genuine repentance always produces a submissive attitude. The person who truly embraces Christ as Savior will also submit to Him as Lord (Luke 6:46). This is the inevitable mark of true saving faith: It involves surrender and submission to the will of God.

No one can expect God's blessing while harboring rebellion or resentment against God in the heart. God has a right to demand our full obedience, and those who willfully and deliberately defy His authority as a pattern of life cannot legitimately claim to have faith in Him who is the supreme Lawgiver.

That means His Word must be the ultimate authority in our lives. Those who want God's blessing must submit to His commands. We cannot plead for divine blessing, if our minds and hearts remain defiant toward His Word.

RESIST THE DEVIL

James's second command goes hand in hand with the first: "Resist the devil" (4:7). Unfortunately, modern American society, by and large, is characterized by *resistance* to God's standards and *tolerance* of the devil's.

In fact, most of our society's values in recent years have been shaped by the devil's agenda. The problem is becoming worse every year as our culture becomes more and more brazen in rejecting the God of Scripture and embracing a devilish worldview.

To cite one example from the popular culture, fifty years ago on television, Ozzie Nelson and family portrayed the average American household on television; but today the highest rated cable television program in history features heavy-metal rocker Ozzy

Osbourne and his quintessentially dysfunctional family. Few realized it when *The Adventures of Ozzie and Harriet* was on the air in the 1950s and '60s, but Ozzie Nelson was a committed atheist. (He later revealed his atheism in an autobiography published in the 1970s.) The '50s sitcom was not overtly anti-Christian, of course, but God was conspicuously absent from the Nelsons' family life. Ozzy Osbourne, on the other hand, makes no secret of his infatuation with Satan, and that is plainly reflected in his family's lifestyle. The road from Ozzie Nelson to Ozzy Osbourne perfectly illustrates how bold society has become in overtly promoting evil and the agenda of the evil one. That is the drift of American culture.

People who truly desire God's blessing must resist the devil and his schemes. That means before we have a right to expect God to bless us, we must turn away from the evil that hinders that blessing. For many Americans—Christians included—that calls for major changes in lifestyle and interests.

The devil and his influence are more prevalent in American culture than most people realize. Scripture says those who practice sin are "of the devil" (1 John 3:8). Jesus told even the religious scribes and Pharisees, "You are of your father the devil, and the desires of your father you want to do" (John 8:44). All who resist God are, in effect, in league with the devil, whether they realize it or not.

But resisting the devil doesn't mean we should declare war on unbelievers. Nor does this call us to engage in the kind of antics some people think constitutes "spiritual warfare"—pretending to command demons, prayer marches, "spiritual mapping," and other superstitious nonsense. It simply means we ourselves must forsake evil, say no to temptation, and refuse everything that would advance the program of the evil one. Above all, we should be alert to the wiles of the devil and fortify ourselves against his deceit and his cunning (Ephesians 6:11) by resisting the father of lies with God's truth.

The Question No One Is Asking

Draw Near to God

Next, James says, we should "draw near to God" (James 4:8). Notice the contrast: "Resist the devil and he will flee from you. Draw near to God and He will draw near to you" (vv. 7–8). Do you want to be blessed by God? Resist the devil and he will flee; and there's certainly ample blessing in that. But an even greater blessing comes in the intimate fellowship we enjoy when we draw near to God, and He draws near to us. His presence sustains us through every trial, comforts us in all our sorrow, strengthens us for every task, communes with us in every quiet moment, and enriches every moment of our lives.

The Psalmist wrote in 73:28, "But it is good for me to draw near to God." In other words, the blessing is inherent in the drawing near. The same psalm celebrates the blessing of God's nearness in verses 23–24: "I am continually with You; You hold me by my right hand. You will guide me with Your counsel, and afterward receive me to glory."

"Drawing near to God" is a familiar biblical expression that speaks of coming to God in humble contrition and reverent worship (cf. 1 Samuel 14:36). It involves an inward motion toward God, not something that can be accomplished by words or religious rituals. In fact, through the prophet Isaiah, the Lord rebukes those who "draw near with their mouths and honor Me with their lips, but have removed their hearts far from Me." Those who would truly draw near to God must come with genuine faith, as Hebrews 10:22 says, "Let us draw near with a true heart in full assurance of faith."

Cleanse Your Hands

The fourth command in James's litany is, "Cleanse your hands, you sinners." This is yet another way of calling for repentance, employing a familiar figure rooted in

Old Testament ceremonial law. Before they came before the Lord to offer sacrifices, priests in the Old Testament went through a ceremony of hand washing (Exodus 30:18–21). This symbolized their recognition that they were sinners who needed cleansing before they could stand in the presence of God.

Isaiah 59:2–3 says, "Your iniquities have separated you from your God. . . . For your hands are defiled with blood, and your fingers with iniquity." Therefore God says, "When you spread out your hands, I will hide My eyes from you; even though you make many prayers, I will not hear. Your hands are full of blood. Wash yourselves, make yourselves clean; put away the evil of your doings from before My eyes. Cease to do evil" (Isaiah 1:15–16).

This is not a call for ceremonial washing in a literal laver of water. What it demands is the putting away of sin, a turning from evil deeds. Again, it is a call for repentance, along with the recognition that sin requires cleansing.

PURIFY YOUR HEARTS

James then employs a parallelism: "and purify your hearts, you double-minded" (James 4:8). Parallelisms like this were used in Hebrew poetry for emphasis. The parallelism simply repeats the same thought in different terms. So "Cleanse your hands, you sinners;" and "purify your hearts, you double-minded" don't express two distinct ideas; both phrases say the same thing in equivalent terms. The expressions "cleanse your hands" and "purify your hearts" both speak of the need for cleansing from guilt. And "you sinners" and "you double-minded" are simply two ways of addressing those in need of repentance.

True cleansing from sin is not something sinners can do for themselves. There is no suggestion in the command "Cleanse your hands . . . and purify your hearts" that sinners have the ability to reform themselves in a way that will gain God's blessing and approval. Scripture is very clear on this. "Can the

Ethiopian change his skin or the leopard its spots? Then may you also do good who are accustomed to do evil" (Jeremiah 13:23). We have no more power to cleanse ourselves from sin than we have to change our skin color. Sin is deeply ingrained in our fallen nature; it is a reflection of our depraved moral character. We cannot, by sheer force of will, change our own character.

But cleansing and complete heart-renewal are works *God* does for those who draw near to Him in faith and with genuine repentance. He says, "I will sprinkle clean water on you, and you shall be clean; I will cleanse you from all your filthiness and from all your idols. I will give you a new heart and put a new spirit within you; I will take the heart of stone out of your flesh and give you a heart of flesh" (Ezekiel 36:25–26). That describes the regeneration of sinners that takes place when we are born again. It is a work God does for us and in us; it is not something we can do for ourselves.

So James underscores the sinner's need for cleansing

and urges his readers to seek that cleansing as they draw near to God.

Lament

James continues, "Lament and mourn and weep!" (James 4:9). He is calling for misery and sorrow and tears over our sin. He employs three verbs without modifiers, and each has its own unique significance.

The first one, "lament," is translated in our English Bible from a Greek expression that speaks of misery and affliction. It describes the heartache we should feel when we realize our own wretchedness as sinners. Perhaps the best New Testament example of this is the tax-collector Jesus described in a parable—the publican who went to the Temple to pray. But sensing his own sinful unworthiness, he did not even dare enter the Temple itself, but "standing afar off, would not so much as raise his eyes to heaven, but beat his breast, saying, 'God, be merciful to me a sinner!'" (Luke 18:13).

The kind of misery that makes us lament our own sinfulness is a necessary condition for true blessing. Jesus said of that tax-collector, "This man went down to his house justified" (v. 14). The Lord Jesus contrasted him with a self-righteous Pharisee whose prayer expressed how good and superior he was compared to others. The Pharisee forfeited blessing because of his smugness and pride. The tax-collector, by contrast, found blessing while in the throes of his own misery.

The misery James calls for is not the typical kind of depression people feel when they are dissatisfied with their lot in life. It has nothing to do with the despondency of self-pity or the lack of contentment felt by those who think life has been unfair to them. It is a misery that stems from a true sense of one's own guilt and a recognition that, because we are sinners, we don't deserve divine blessing. It is the cry of the heart that knows it has offended the righteousness of God and has no hope apart from God's mercy.

MOURN

"Mourn" is the next imperative in this series of three stand-alone verbs. This moves beyond the idea of pain and anguish and speaks of the deep grief and remorse that comes with understanding how sinful we are and feeling our own responsibility for our guilt.

It is an irony that the pathway to true blessing takes us through misery and mourning. In fact, the idea of mourning may seem at first glance to be the polar opposite of blessing. But Christ taught everywhere that the necessary prelude to genuine blessing is a sense of sorrow and misery over our own sinfulness. The second Beatitude is "Blessed are those who mourn, for they shall be comforted" (Matthew 5:4). He was speaking of those who mourn over their sinfulness—people whose own sin makes them profoundly sorrowful.

An illustration of this is the reaction of Isaiah, when he saw a vision of God in His glory. His immediate response was mourning. He said, "Woe is me, for I am undone! Because I am a man of unclean lips, and I dwell in the midst of a people of unclean lips; for my eyes have seen the King, the LORD of hosts" (Isaiah 6:5). The reality of his sin caused him woe, and that is precisely the kind of mourning for which James is calling.

WEEP

Not only misery and mourning, but also tears should be our response when we realize and confess our sinfulness. Weeping is the natural manifestation of true misery and mourning.

That is how Peter responded on the night of Jesus' betrayal after he had denied Christ three times. Christ had foretold his failure, but Peter had expressed confidence that he would never deny his Lord. Jesus told him, "Assuredly, I say to you that today, even this night, before the rooster crows twice, you will deny Me three times" (Mark 14:30).

Later that night, in fear for his life and threatened

with exposure while watching Jesus stand trial, Peter "began to curse and swear, 'I do not know this Man of whom you speak!'" (v. 71).

What a devastating failure that was for Peter! What a shameful way for a disciple to behave! But to Peter's credit, he recognized his guilt immediately. Instantly, when he denied Christ for the third time, Scripture says, "A second time the rooster crowed. Then Peter called to mind the word that Jesus had said to him, 'Before the rooster crows twice, you will deny Me three times.' And when he thought about it, *he wept*" (v. 72, emphasis added). Matthew 26:75 and Luke 22:62 say he "wept bitterly."

Peter's tears were not like Esau's (Hebrews 12:17). After bartering away his birthright and the blessing that went with it, Esau wept and pleaded to get it back. The difference is that Peter mourned over his sin; Esau was mourning over the consequences of his sin. As the apostle Paul wrote in 2 Corinthians 7:10, "Godly sorrow produces repentance leading to salvation, not to be regretted; but the sorrow of the world produces death." Our misery, our mourning, and our tears must flow from true sorrow over the *fact* of our sin, not a superficial regret over sin's *consequences*.

Get Serious

James's ninth imperative continues the thought of the previous three: "Let your laughter be turned to mourning and your joy to gloom" (James 4:9). He is not calling for an outlook on life that is always and only gloomy. He is not condemning laughter and joy in every context. In fact, Christians are supposed to be joyful (Philippians 1:25; 2:17–18).

But in this context, James is describing an attitude of repentance. He is teaching that when we contemplate our own sin, it ought to make us sorrowful, sober, and serious-minded.

We live in a society that rarely takes anything seriously, especially the reality of sin and personal guilt.

25

James's point is that those who desire the blessing of God ought to view their own sin with the utmost sorrow and sobriety. Life in a sinful world cannot and should not always be filled with laughter and mirth. Sin is serious, and it ought to be contemplated seriously. Those who realize their sin and mourn will be comforted (Matthew 5:4), but the mourning is the necessary prelude to the blessing of divine comfort. We have no legitimate right to ask for divine blessing until we have contemplated our sin in all seriousness.

When Jeremiah thought about the sin of his people, he wrote, "The joy of our heart has ceased; Our dance has turned into mourning. The crown has fallen from our head. Woe to us, for we have sinned!" (Lamentations 5:15). Such an attitude is one of the necessary conditions for God's blessing on any people.

Humble Yourselves

James's final command sums up all the others: "Humble yourselves in the sight of the Lord, and He will lift you

up" (James 4:10). This is the humility of genuine repentance. How do we humble ourselves? Through all the
means James has just listed: Submit to God, resist the
devil, draw near to God, cleanse your hands, purify your
hearts, lament, mourn, weep, and get into a serious
frame of mind about your sin.

James preceded this list of ten imperatives by saying,
"God resists the proud, but gives grace to the humble"
(v. 6). He was quoting from the Greek translation of
Proverbs 3:34: "Surely He scorns the scornful, but gives
grace to the humble."

That sums up all the conditions for receiving divine
blessing in a simple statement.

Can God bless America? Yes, but if we are to be the
recipients of His blessing, *we* must be humble and
repentant over our own sin. God resists those who revel
in pride and arrogance; He exalts those who humble
themselves. Calamities such as those that have struck
our nation could be harbingers of greater judgments to
come, or they could be the prelude to divine blessing.
The difference will be seen in how we respond.

2

Bring the Book!

"Now all the people gathered together as one man in the open square that was in front of the Water Gate; and they told Ezra the scribe to bring the Book of the Law of Moses, which the Lord had commanded Israel."
—NEHEMIAH 8:1

Rebellion, the sexual revolution, and secular humanism have dominated American life since the 1960s. Numerous Christian leaders have warned repeatedly that if God does *not* judge America, He will have to apologize to Sodom and Gomorrah. Indeed, God plainly threatens judgment against nations that turn against His truth. "'If they do not obey, I will utterly pluck up and destroy that nation,' says the LORD" (Jeremiah 12:17). Perhaps no society has ever taken a more dramatic turn against God than America did in the latter half of the twentieth century. Divine judgment seems inevitable if our nation continues down that road.

But judgment can still be averted and blessing regained through repentance and spiritual renewal. The word of the Lord through the prophet Jeremiah goes on to say, "The instant I speak concerning a nation and concerning a kingdom, to pluck up, to pull down, and to destroy it, if that nation against whom I have spoken turns from its evil, I will relent of the disaster that I thought to bring upon it" (18:7–8).

Certainly God can bless America, but the necessary prelude to national blessing is a sweeping spiritual renewal that begins with individual repentance and faith in the Lord Jesus Christ. Apart from a such a profound spiritual awakening and a decisive return to the God of Scripture, we have no right as a nation to anticipate anything *but* God's judgment.

The revival our nation needs so badly will not occur unless we as *individuals* repent. Authentic repentance involves a change of heart, not merely a change of public policy. And the *first* to repent must be the people of God—Christians who know and love Christ but who have fallen into a state of spiritual lethargy or indifference and have left their first love (cf. Rev. 2:4). We have diverted our efforts and energies and strategies from evangelism. We need to repent of that.

Unfortunately, the church today is at war with the culture, and many Christians think that by opposing moral decline through protest and politics, they are doing all they can do to redeem society. They have begun to view their unbelieving neighbors as the enemy rather than the mission field. As the rift widens between the Religious Right and the rest of society, the gospel message is being lost in the din of conflict. The tender love of sinners has been replaced by bitter rivalry for influence. Thus the only truth that can ultimately draw people to sincere repentance is too often being set aside in favor of political rhetoric and partisan squabbling.

No national revival has ever occurred because of political strategizing or legislative initiatives. Revivals don't occur when the people of God protest and demonstrate against the sins of unbelievers. Revivals aren't the fruit of boycotts or debates about public policy. Revivals occur when the Word of God is proclaimed and people are called to repentance. This was true in Nineveh, when an entire city of pagans responded to the preaching of Jonah by repenting in sackcloth and ashes (Jonah 3:5–10). It was true at Pentecost, when thousands in Jerusalem suddenly repented. They were the very same people who had demanded the crucifixion of Christ a few weeks earlier. But when Peter preached the gospel to them in the power of the Holy Spirit at Pentecost, they received the Word of God and were added to the church (Acts 2:41). That is how revivals invariably occur. That is exactly what happened in the Great Awakening, when our nation's forefathers repented under the passionate, relentless preaching of men like Jonathan Edwards and George Whitefield. Study the history of revival, and you will discover that this has always been the case. Revival comes in response to the clear and forceful preaching of God's Word out of hearts filled with love for the lost.

HEARTS PREPARED FOR GOD'S BLESSING

Scripture records still another great national revival that occurred in response to the preaching of God's Word during the time of Nehemiah. At that particular point in Israel's history, the people were returning to their homeland after a long period of divine judgment and exile. Their days of captivity were finally at an end. They were craving the blessing of God on their nation. Their land was filled with rubble. Their city and its walls were torn down. The temple had already been rebuilt by early returnees a generation earlier. But the city itself was still in ruins, and it was destined to remain in ruins as long as it had no walls. The walls were finally rebuilt under Nehemiah's leadership.

But the people still longed for God's blessing. The rebuilding of the wall alone wasn't enough. The rebuilding of the rest of the city still needed to be undertaken. But the people sensed an even greater need: Their own personal lives and the very spirit of their nation also needed rebuilding. So before they even began reconstructing their houses (Nehemiah 7:4), they convened together to hear the Word of God. It was then that revival occurred. The most significant and meaningful blessing of God came in response to the proclamation of His Word.

Nehemiah describes the scene: "All the people gathered together as one man in the open square that was in front of the Water Gate; and they told Ezra the scribe to bring the Book of the Law of Moses, which the LORD had commanded Israel" (Nehemiah 8:1). They were united in purpose and expectation. They had one aim: They wanted to hear from God. They desired God's blessing, and they understood that before they could have His blessing, they needed to hear what God demanded of *them*.

So they brought out the Book. They were eager to hear the Scriptures. "Ezra the priest brought the Law before the assembly of men and women and all who could hear with understanding on the first day of the seventh month. Then he read from it in the open square that was in front of the Water Gate from morning until midday, before the men and women and those who could understand; and the ears of all the people were attentive to the Book of the Law" (vv. 2–3).

Ezra read for hours—from morning until midday—and the people remained attentive. They had planned and prepared for this day. Verse 4 says, "Ezra the scribe stood on a platform of wood which they had made for the purpose." It was an elevated platform, so that everyone could see (v. 5). And to show their reverence, "when he opened [the Book], all the people stood up."

Their hearts were prepared. They had looked forward to this day. They listened attentively, while standing the whole time. And Ezra both read and explained the text. Verse 8 says, "They read distinctly from the book, in the Law of God; and they gave the sense, and helped them to understand the reading." That is a fine description of what all good preaching ought to be. They read the text distinctly, explained the sense of it, and helped the people understand.

If You Love God, Keep His Commandments

The reading of the Law went on for days. Verses 13–14 describe how, on the second day of the reading, they found where Moses had commanded the people to observe the Feast of Tabernacles during the seventh month. It happened to be the seventh month at that very time (7:73; 8:2). So the people instantly responded by observing the feast.

The Feast of Tabernacles was Israel's harvest feast, a joyous celebration at the end of every harvest. It also commemorated the commencement of the Israelites' journey through the wilderness on the way from Egypt to Canaan. During the week of the feast, the Israelites would build temporary shelters—booths—out of small branches, "the fruit of beautiful trees, branches of palm trees, the boughs of leafy trees, and willows of the brook" (Leviticus 23:40). Families moved into their booths and lived there for the entire seven days of the feast.

God had meant the feast to be a time of joy and celebration. Living in the booths was supposed to remind them of God's fatherly care during their wilderness wanderings. As a celebration of harvest, the festival also reminded them of God's provision.

When Ezra had begun reading from the Book, however, the initial response of the people was grief, not gladness. "For all the people wept, when they heard the words of the Law" (Nehemiah 8:9). They were weighed down by the realization of their own guilt. Ezra and Nehemiah had to tell them to rejoice, and not weep, because their hearts were moved with such contrition upon hearing the words of the Law. Nehemiah told them, "Go your way, eat the fat, drink the sweet, and send portions to those for whom nothing is prepared; for this day is holy to our LORD. Do not sorrow, for the joy of the LORD is your strength" (v. 10).

So they celebrated the Feast of Tabernacles with joy, as the Word of God commanded. Nehemiah says,

> Then the people went out and brought them and made themselves booths, each one on the roof of his house, or in their courtyards or the courts of the house of God, and in the open square of the Water Gate and in the open square of the Gate of Ephraim. So the whole assembly of those who had returned from the captivity made booths and sat under the booths; for since the days of Joshua the son of Nun until that day the children of Israel had not done so. *And there was very great gladness* (vv. 16–17, emphasis added).

Notice that their immediate response to everything they heard was obedience.

And the reading and preaching of God's Word

continued through the days of the feast: "Also day by day, from the first day until the last day, he read from the Book of the Law of God. And they kept the feast seven days; and on the eighth day there was a sacred assembly, according to the prescribed manner" (v. 18). Day after day, they read the Word while the people stood and gratefully listened.

LET YOUR LAUGHTER BE TURNED INTO MOURNING

But throughout those joyful days of the festival, the people apparently retained the awareness that they had unfinished business with the Lord. They needed to express their repentance. And so, in Nehemiah 9:1, we read, "Now on the twenty-fourth day of this month the children of Israel were assembled with fasting, in sackcloth, and with dust on their heads." As soon as the celebratory festival was over, they covered themselves with sackcloth and ashes.

That was the posture and the attire of penitence and humiliation. Their hearts were filled with an awareness of their own sinfulness, and they knew they needed to express their repentance and mourn over their sin.

And now they began to obey the law of God in earnest. Verse 2 says, "Then those of Israelite lineage separated themselves from all foreigners; and they stood and confessed their sins and the iniquities of their fathers." They confessed their sins, both personal and corporate. They clearly recognized that sin was the very reason their nation had endured such a prolonged captivity. So they postured themselves as penitents, then confessed their own sins, as well as the sins and iniquities of their fathers. "And they stood up in their place and read from the Book of the Law of the LORD their God for one-fourth of the day; and for another fourth they confessed and worshiped the LORD their God" (v. 3). Thus they continued being attentive to the Word, even when they could no longer delay expressing their repentance.

Here we see what it looks like when the people of God place themselves by the prompting of God into a position to be blessed. Bring the Book. Read the law of God. Confess that you have disobeyed it. And God will bless you. That is the pattern of blessing.

The rest of Nehemiah 9 is the record of the prayer offered to God by the people of Israel that day. They started with praise to God as the Creator and Sovereign Lord of the universe (v. 6). Then they recounted the history of their nation, from the call of Abraham to the Babylonian captivity (vv. 7–30). The focal point of Israel's history was the covenant God made with Abraham (v. 8). Moreover, the whole point of reciting Israel's history was to show that God had always been faithful to His covenant, but the Israelites had not. They had broken the covenant repeatedly and transgressed the Law of God throughout their history.

In fact, the closing section of the prayer contrasts the grace and mercy of God as a covenant-keeping God with the sin and rebellion of His covenant-breaking people:

Nevertheless in Your great mercy You did not utterly consume them nor forsake them; for You are God, gracious and merciful. Now therefore, our God, the great, the mighty, and awesome God, Who keeps covenant and mercy: Do not let all the trouble seem small before You that has come upon us, our kings and our princes, our priests and our prophets, our fathers and on all Your people, from the days of the kings of Assyria until this day. However You are just in all that has befallen us; for You have dealt faithfully, but we have done wickedly. Neither our kings nor our princes, our priests nor our fathers, have kept Your law, nor heeded Your commandments and Your testimonies, with which You testified against them. For they have not served You in their kingdom, or in the many good things that You gave them, or in the large and rich land which You set before them; nor did they turn from their wicked works. Here we are, servants today! And the land that You gave to our fathers, to eat its fruit and its bounty, here we are, servants in it! And it yields much increase to the kings You have set over us, because of our sins; also they have dominion over our bodies and our cattle at their pleasure; and we are in great distress. (vv. 31–37)

Then they closed by renewing the covenant: "And because of all this, we make a sure covenant, and write it; our leaders, our Levites, and our priests seal it" (v. 38).

They confessed that they had been admonished to turn back to God's law. Yet the nation had acted arrogantly. They had ignored God's commandments, sinned against His ordinances, "shrugged their shoulders, stiffened their necks, and would not hear" (v. 29).

Israel knew there was no mystery to the conditions for divine blessing. They had a covenant with God that spelled out exactly what God expected of them. But as a nation and as individuals, they had broken the covenant; they had sinned; and now their only hope for regaining God's blessing was to confess their sin, admit their guilt, and cast themselves on His mercy. But because He is a covenant-keeping God, they knew they could trust Him for the promised mercy.

They *did* receive great blessing from the hand of God. The recovery of God's Word alone was a great blessing. And as the people submitted to the Word of God and lived their lives in a way that reflected their repentance, a new era of recovery and prosperity swept over Israel. That generation of Israelites enjoyed tremendous peace and prosperity under Nehemiah's leadership.

Sadly, it was not long before the people began to compromise in small ways. The closing chapter of Nehemiah's account describes how his duties to the king of Babylon required him to leave Jerusalem for a time (Nehemiah 13:6). In his absence, the people of Jerusalem began to forget about obedience to God's law. One of the nation's bitterest enemies was given a room in the Temple courts (v. 7). The priests of the Temple were not given the share of the land that was due them (v. 10). The Sabbath was being profaned (v. 15). Israelites had begun marrying unbelievers (v. 23). Even some priests were defiling the priesthood by marrying pagans (vv. 28–29). When Nehemiah discovered these things, he corrected them. He knew what many believers often forget: Constant reform is necessary if the people of God are going to remain faithful. People are always fickle. But God's mercy is not.

God is still the same today. He "is gracious and full of compassion, slow to anger and great in mercy" (Psalm 145:8). He is "good, and ready to forgive, and abundant in mercy to all those who call upon [Him]" (Psalm 86:5). "The LORD is good; His mercy is everlasting, and His truth endures to all generations" (Psalm 100:5). "The LORD, the LORD, the compassionate and gracious God, slow to anger, abounding in love and faithfulness, maintaining love to thousands, and forgiving wickedness, rebellion and sin" (Exodus 34:6–7).

Unlike ancient Israel, America is not a covenant nation. God has made no promise to our physical ancestors that guarantees our national status forever. If Israel had to fulfill the conditions for divine blessing, even though God had covenanted with them as His chosen people, America certainly has no inviolable claim on the blessing of God. As long as unbelief and disobedience to the Word of God color the soul of our nation, we simply cannot expect the blessing of God. Israel didn't get it in her unbelief.

But for those of us who are Christians, the covenant blessings *do* apply. "If you are Christ's, then you are Abraham's seed, and heirs according to the promise" (Galatians 3:29). All the promises of salvation, mercy, forgiveness for our sins, and spiritual prosperity are ours to claim as long as we remain faithful to God.

That is why the spiritual state of the church in our nation is the key to the blessing of the nation as a whole. If God is going to bless America, it will not be for the sake of the nation itself. He blesses the nation, and has always done so, for the sake of His people. If we who are called by His name are not fulfilling the conditions for divine blessing, there is no hope whatsoever for the rest of the nation.

On the other hand, if the church is fit to receive God's blessing, the whole nation will be the beneficiary of that, because the Word of God will be proclaimed with power, God will add to His church, and spiritual blessings of all kinds will result. And those are the truest blessings of all.

Scripture says, "Judgment must begin at the house of God" (1 Peter 4:17, KJV). It is equally true that blessing begins with the people of God, and it spills over from there. That is the one true hope for real blessing on our nation.

3

COMING TO GRIPS WITH OUR GUILT

Why, O Lord, do you stand far off?
Why do you hide yourself in times of trouble?
—Psalm 10:1

Americans do not like the concept of guilt. Guilt feelings are regarded as a symptom of weakness and low self-esteem. Our culture has decided that guilt is counterproductive, emotionally hurtful, and too negative. Many would prefer to do away with the concept altogether.

For example, advice columnist Ann Landers wrote, "One of the most painful, self-mutilating, time- and energy-consuming exercises in the human experience is guilt. . . . Guilt is a pollutant and we don't need any more of it in the world."[1] In his best-selling book *Your*

Erroneous Zones, Dr. Wayne Dyer called guilt "a futile waste of time." Dismissing guilt as a neurosis—a mental disorder—he said, "Guilt is the most useless of all behaviors. It is by far the greatest waste of emotional energy. Guilt zones must be exterminated, spray-cleaned and sterilized forever."[2]

People want their sin, but they don't want the guilt it produces. And so they live in denial.

THE DANGER OF TRUTH-DENIAL

Deliberately denying or suppressing guilt is a sure pathway to judgment and distress, not blessing. God made the human soul with a conscience so that we can feel the effects of our sin and be aware of the fact that we are guilty. The conscience is the spiritual counterpart of our physical pain sensors, which let us know when we are sick or in danger of serious injury. In other words, the conscience itself actually *is* one of God's blessings. And therefore those who ignore or suppress their guilt have *already* deliberately forfeited divine blessing.

The long-term effects of denying guilt are spiritually deadly. Deny your guilt long enough or completely enough, and you must also deny God himself. Those who destroy their consciences render themselves mentally and morally unfit for making right judgments. In such a state, they utterly cut themselves off from divine blessing. There is no remedy for the guilt of those who have eliminated their own consciences.

We see clearly an outline of this process in the opening chapters of Paul's epistle to the Romans. The apostle is making the argument that all humanity is under the curse of sin. No race, nation, or individual is guilt-free before God. The climax of his point comes in Romans 3:10: "There is none righteous, no, not one." All are guilty.

Paul begins this line of argument in Romans 1 by recounting the steps of humanity's descent into sin and judgment. He writes, "The wrath of God is revealed from heaven against all ungodliness and unrighteousness of men, who suppress the truth in unrighteousness, because what may be known of God is manifest in them, for God has shown it to them" (Romans 1:18–19).

Notice, first, that divine wrath, not blessing, is the inevitable result when we suppress the truth. It may feel good in a temporal sense to deny our guilt and to put out of our thoughts the truth that we are accountable to God, but this is a sure pathway to destruction.

Notice also that God has already revealed truth about Himself in every human heart. We as humans are created in the image of God. Our rational faculties and our moral capacity are patterned after God's own mind. The stamp of His likeness is imprinted on our souls, and along with it we have an inherent understanding that God exists. Our own conscience tells us He does exist, and we are accountable to Him. That is why we feel guilt in the first place.

Everything we see in God's creation gives us some

basic knowledge of what He is like. "For since the creation of the world His invisible attributes are clearly seen, being understood by the things that are made, even His eternal power and Godhead" (v. 20). All creation testifies to the glory and omnipotence of God. It gives evidence of His goodness, His love for beauty, His limitless intelligence, His eternality, and His kindness to His creatures. All those truths about God are clearly discernable in nature, whether we look at the stars in a telescope, at a drop of pond water in a microscope, or simply at all the scenery around us. Evidence of God's glory and greatness is everywhere. According to Scripture we are "without excuse" (v. 20) if we ignore that evidence.

Furthermore, according to Romans 2:14–15, the moral law of God is built right into the fabric of our souls: "For when Gentiles, who do not have the law, by nature do the things in the law, these, although not having the law, are a law to themselves, who show the work of *the law written in their hearts*, their conscience also bearing witness" (emphasis added). So some basic knowledge of God and His moral standards is written on each one of our hearts and attested to by our consciences.

But because we are sinful, it is the natural tendency of all of us to suppress that truth. Romans 1:21–23 traces the path of humanity's decline into sin: "Although they knew God, they did not glorify Him as God, nor were thankful, but became futile in their thoughts, and their foolish hearts were darkened. Professing to be wise, they became fools, and changed the glory of the incorruptible God into an image made like corruptible man; and birds and four-footed animals and creeping things."

That means the inevitable end of truth—suppression is idolatry, the violation of the First Commandment: "You shall have no other gods before Me" (Exodus 20:3). According to Scripture, monotheism did not evolve from lower forms of polytheistic religion; actually, polytheism and idolatry represent the *devolution* of humanity's innate spiritual understanding.

They are the result of suppressing the truth that is inherent in the human heart.

Romans 1 sets forth precisely the path our nation has followed in its spiritual decline. We in America have always had access to more than just the truth of God that is imbedded in the human heart and emblazoned on creation (*general* revelation). Our nation also has easy access to the written Word of God in Scripture (*special* revelation).

In fact, the first European settlements to be planted on this continent were all Bible-believing communities that had grown out of the Puritan movement in England. They were devoted to building a society that reflected the truth of God's Word. To this day, we have God in our flag salute; we have His name on our coins; we sing of Him in our songs. But the overwhelming majority of modern Americans simply do not have Him in their minds or their hearts. The problem is that as a nation, we have known God, but we do not glorify Him as God, nor are we thankful to Him (v. 21).

According to this passage, when people remove God from their consciousness, ban His name from public discussion, and make Him politically incorrect, the inevitable result is that all their thinking becomes futile, and their foolish hearts are darkened. Professing to be wise, they become fools (v. 22). The Greek word translated "fools" there is *moraino*— literally, "simpletons." It is the root of the English word *morons*.

The next step on the downward path is rank idolatry, where God is replaced by an image in the likeness of humanity, beasts, and even creeping things. Has that happened in America? Certainly. Society is filled with people who follow human gurus as if they were gods. Others practice a narcissistic worship of their own bodies, or devote their lives to other forms of self-adulation. Many environmentalists worship creation, consumed with dolphins, or spotted owls, or even trees. Examine eco-feminism, or any other New-Age religion, and you will find idolatry that is every bit as profane as any kind of Old Testament paganism. Our nation has pursued precisely the same path Paul outlined in Romans 1.

It is not just an American problem, however. Paul is showing in Romans 1 that this is the whole course of human history. Every nation has gone this way. Examine Western Europe, for example, where the gospel first spread and from which it went out to the rest of the world. Europe was also the birthplace of the Protestant Reformation less than 500 years ago. On the heels of Luther and Calvin was a revival of biblical faith the likes of which the world had never seen. But Western Europe today is a spiritual wasteland, overrun with agnosticism, humanism, and widespread ignorance of God's Word. Europe followed the path described in Romans 1 step by step. And America is nearing the end of that path in our generation.

What Does God's Wrath Look Like?

Now look again at how Paul begins this whole discussion in Romans 1:18: "For the wrath of God is revealed from heaven" against all who pursue this path of truth-suppression and idolatry. *Wrath*, certainly not blessing, is the result when a society suppresses the knowledge of God and suppresses the testimony of the human conscience.

What does divine wrath look like? The apostle Paul describes God's wrath beginning in verses 24–25, and he is very specific: "Therefore God also gave them up to uncleanness, in the lusts of their hearts, to dishonor their bodies among themselves, who exchanged the truth of God for the lie, and worshiped and served the creature rather than the Creator." He repeats the same idea in verse 26: "God gave them up to vile passions." And again he says it in verse 28: "God gave them over to a debased mind."

What is the most fearful expression of divine wrath

a society can face? It is this: God gives them over to their own sin. He abandons them to whatever they love. They love uncleanness? God abandons them to that. They love vile passions? God gives them up to homosexuality and perversions of all kinds (vv. 26–27).

That is a fitting description of what has happened in America in the past generation. We are seeing the effects of God's wrath. Notice carefully the steps of decline Paul outlines in Romans 1. When a nation abandons God and turns to idols, God abandons them (Romans 1:24). First, they sink to immorality (v. 24). Then they sink deeper to homosexuality (vv. 26–27). So they start by embracing heterosexual sin, and then they turn to homosexual sin. Does anyone question that we are already there?

But there's another step in the declension, described in verse 28: "God gave them over to a debased mind." The Greek word translated "debased" is *adokimos*. It speaks of something useless, spurned, and reprobate. The mind becomes spiritually useless—morally incapable of making a right judgment. And when a society has gone that far, there is no way back. You know society is reaching that point when people will not tolerate anyone making moral judgments.

When people love and revel in things that are debased and depraved and twisted, God leaves them to what they love—"to do those things which are not fitting." And when their minds finally do become incapable of making moral judgments, there is no help for them—"being filled with all unrighteousness, sexual immorality, wickedness, covetousness, maliciousness; full of envy, murder, strife, deceit, evil-mindedness; they are whisperers, backbiters, haters of God, violent, proud, boasters, inventors of evil things, disobedient to parents, undiscerning, untrustworthy, unloving, unforgiving, unmerciful" (vv. 28–31).

Scripture says when a society descends to that point, they give approval to sin even though they know such sins are destructive to society and damning to the individual. All sense of guilt is finally eradicated. Knowing that death is the result of such practices, people nonetheless accept such things and even give hearty approval to those who do them: "Knowing the righteous judgment of God, that those who practice such things are deserving of death, not only do the same but also approve of those who practice them" (v. 32).

At that point, all hope for the society is gone. Media and public discourse become vile and profane. *The Jerry Springer Show* becomes high entertainment in such a culture. The approval rating for an immoral politician skyrockets. That is what divine wrath looks like.

God's wrath is portrayed many ways in Scripture. There is *eternal* wrath—everlasting punishment in hell. There is *apocalyptic* wrath—the massive disasters and calamities that will unfold at the end of the age, described in the Book of Revelation. There are occasional incidents of *cataclysmic* wrath, such as the flood in Noah's day or the destruction that fell on the cities of Sodom and Gomorrah. There are *natural* manifestations of divine wrath built into the consequences of sin. (For example, if you sin by abusing drugs or alcohol, the natural effects of that sin can destroy your body, your family life, your reputation, or ultimately your whole earthly existence. That's the sowing and reaping principle at work [cf. Galatians 6:7–8]).

But what Paul is describing in Romans 1 is a totally different expression of divine wrath. This is *the wrath of abandonment*. It is a frightening reality. God gives people over completely to their own sinful desires, steps back, and lets them go. They want their sin, so God allows them to have it without hindrance. He simply withdraws the blessing of His restraining grace.

THE COMPLACENCY OF FOOLS

Scripture is filled with accounts of individuals and societies who were given up by God to their own sin and its consequences. Judges 16, for example, gives a classic example. That chapter describes how Samson became romantically infatuated with a Philistine woman, Delilah. Samson had been involved with Philistine women before. He had married one in disobedience to God and his parents, and that union almost destroyed him (Judges 14:1—15:8). His failed marriage caused him constant conflict with the Philistines (15:8–15). Next, he indulged in an illicit affair with a Philistine prostitute, and that also exposed him to further attack by the Philistines (16:1–3).

Finally, he allowed himself to be seduced by Delilah. She began cajoling him to get him to tell her the secret of his strength. Three times he lied to her. First he told her he could be bound with fresh bowstrings. Then he said he could be bound only by unused ropes. Then he told her if she wove his hair into a loom, that would render him helpless. Each time Delilah bound him by the method he suggested, and she conspired with Philistine warriors to attack him while he was bound. He should have known she was in league with his enemies, but he did not care. Each time he simply broke the bonds and overcame his Philistine attackers.

Apparently, this became a game to Samson. Perhaps he began to think he was truly invincible. So he carried on his carnal romance with Delilah, and Scripture says, "She pestered him daily with her words and pressed him, so that his soul was vexed to death" (16:16). Finally, "He told her all his heart, and said to her, 'No razor has ever come upon my head, for I have been a Nazirite to God from my mother's womb. If I am shaven, then my strength will leave me, and I shall become weak, and be like any other man'" (v. 17).

Samson's devotion to the Lord was signified by the Nazirite vow he had lived under since he was a child in his mother's womb. Among other things, that vow forbade him to cut his hair. The strength wasn't really in his hair; it was from the Lord—a supernatural manifestation of the Spirit of God who indwelt him. But his hair represented the one part of the Nazirite vow Samson had never broken. Cutting it would represent the final act of disobedience in a life that had been marked by apostasy and self-indulgence.

Scripture tells us Delilah "lulled him to sleep on her knees, and called for a man and had him shave off the seven locks of his head" (v. 19). Then as she began to try to awaken him from his sleep, Scripture says, "his strength left him." The Lord abandoned Samson to his sin at that point. "And [Delilah] said, 'The Philistines are upon you, Samson!' So he awoke from his sleep, and said, 'I will go out as before, at other times, and shake myself free!' But *he did not know that the* LORD *had departed from him*" (v. 20, emphasis added).

What is most tragic about the situation is that Samson did not even realize the Lord had abandoned him as he slept on Delilah's lap. He awoke thinking he could do what he had always done. But "the Philistines took him and put out his eyes, and brought him down to Gaza. They bound him with bronze fetters, and he became a grinder in the prison" (v. 21). The physical blindness was a fitting symbol of the spiritual blindness he had willfully brought upon himself. Samson's sin cost him his freedom, his eyes, his dignity, and ultimately his life.

In a similar way, God also abandoned the whole nation of Israel to their sin during the era of the Judges. He told them, "You have forsaken Me and served other gods. Therefore I will deliver you no more. Go and cry out to the gods which you have chosen; let them deliver you in your time of distress" (Judges 10:13–14). He was done with them. They had chosen other gods. Let *those* gods deliver Israel. The people had abandoned God; now He would abandon them.

In Hosea 4:17, the prophet said, "Ephraim is joined to idols, let him alone." Jesus made a similar remark about the Pharisees in Matthew 15:14: "Let them alone. They are blind leaders of the blind. And if the blind leads the blind, both will fall into a ditch."

That's the frightening wrath of God, when He just steps back and leaves sinners to become spiritually inebriated with their own sins.

In Proverbs 1:24–32, God speaks as the personification of wisdom. He says,

Because I have called and you refused, I have stretched out my hand and no one regarded, because you disdained all my counsel, and would have none of my rebuke, I also will laugh at your calamity; I will mock when your terror comes, When your terror comes like a storm, and your destruction comes like a whirlwind, when distress and anguish come upon you.

Then they will call on me, but I will not answer; they will seek me diligently, but they will not find me. Because they hated knowledge and did not choose the fear of the LORD, They would have none of my counsel and despised my every rebuke. Therefore they shall eat the fruit of their own way, and be filled to the full with their own fancies. For the turning away of the simple will slay them, and the complacency of fools will destroy them.

Is that not an apt description of our nation? Will the complacency of fools destroy us? Are we saying futilely against a vaulted sky, "God bless America" when God is not going to answer? Are we on the precipice of being utterly abandoned by God?

Think about it: On what basis could God bless our nation in its current state? America has turned its back on God, rejected His holy Law, followed other gods, and indulged in the grossest kinds of immorality. There is no reason at all why God should bless this nation presently, and there are plenty of reasons why He should turn it over to the consequences of its own wickedness. At this point, just singing a song or displaying a bumper sticker certainly will not procure His blessing.

IS THERE STILL HOPE?

But listen again to God's pleadings with the nation of Israel. In 2 Chronicles 7, after Solomon had finished the dedication of the first temple in Jerusalem, the Lord appeared to him at night and told him, "When I shut up heaven and there is no rain, or command the locusts to devour the land, or send pestilence among My people, if My people who are called by My name will humble themselves, and pray and seek My face, and turn from their wicked ways, then I will hear from heaven, and will forgive their sin and heal their land" (vv. 13–14).

Obviously, that was a covenant promise specifically for Israel. But, again, the principle is true for the people of God for all time. We who are Christ's "are Abraham's seed, and heirs according to the promise" (Galatians 3:29). That means even the promise of 2 Chronicles 7:14 has a valid application for Christians. "For all the promises of God in [Christ] are Yes, and in Him Amen, to the glory of God through us" (2 Corinthians 1:20).

Similarly, in Psalm 81:13–14, God says, "Oh, that My people would listen to Me, that Israel would walk in My ways! I would soon subdue their enemies, and turn My hand against their adversaries." Obviously, the best hope for *any* nation to be safe, secure, free, and prosperous is to walk in the Lord's ways and let Him subdue their enemies.

God went on to tell Israel "He would have fed them also with the finest of wheat; and with honey from the rock I would have satisfied you" (v. 16). The way to have God's best is to turn from our sin and walk in His ways. That is true blessing.

Christians in America must lead the way back to God. We must confess our guilt, revive our consciences, turn from our sin, and turn to God. Then we must boldly proclaim the way of blessing to those who do not know Christ. "Oh, taste and see that the LORD is good; blessed is the man who trusts in Him!" (Psalm 34:8).

Jesus Christ is the only way to God (John 14:6). "Nor is there salvation in any other, for there is no other name under heaven given among men by which we must be saved" (Acts 4:12). Christ alone holds the solution for human guilt.

How is Christ the answer to human guilt? The answer to that question is the gospel message: Christ is God (John 1:1), but He came to earth as a man (v. 14)—fully human and fully God—in order to become the one mediator between God and men (1 Timothy 2:5).

He alone of all humanity was entirely sinless throughout His life. He "is holy, harmless, undefiled, separate from sinners" (Hebrews 7:26). He "was in all points tempted as we are, yet without sin" (4:15). He "'committed no sin, nor was deceit found in His mouth; who, when He was reviled, did not revile in return; when He suffered, He did not threaten, but committed Himself to Him who judges righteously" (1 Peter 2:22–23). He lived a perfect life, the only person ever to have done so. He alone had no guilt of His own.

Yet even though Christ Himself was perfectly sinless, He bore the penalty of sin on behalf of all who trust Him. That was the whole point of His coming to earth in the first place—"to put away sin by the sacrifice of Himself" (Hebrews 9:26). Scripture says, "[God] made Him who knew no sin to be sin for us, that we might become the righteousness of God in Him" (2 Corinthians 5:21). In other words, God imputed the guilt of sinners to His own sinless Son, and then punished Him for it on the cross. The righteousness of Christ is therefore imputed to all who believe (Romans 4:4–6), and God blesses them for it. To put it in plain language, God treated Christ as if he had lived my sinful, guilty life, so that He could treat me as if I had lived Christ's perfect, sinless life. That is the great truth of substitution—the gospel message. It speaks of the greatest blessing God can ever bestow on anyone. It promises eternal blessing to all who trust in Christ alone.

This is the one and only remedy for guilt. Denial and guilt-suppression are the pathway to wrath and judgment. But if we confess our sins and embrace Christ, who alone has atoned for sin, "He is faithful and just to forgive us our sins and to cleanse us from all unrighteousness" (1 John 1:9). Here is the true pathway to the greatest blessing of all.

Psalm 32:1–2 says, "Blessed is he whose transgression is forgiven, whose sin is covered. Blessed is the man to whom the LORD does not impute iniquity." Ultimate blessing—and the key to all God's promised blessings—is provided through Jesus Christ and Him alone. That blessing can be yours by simple faith in Christ, for "whoever calls on the name of the LORD shall be saved" (Romans 10:13).

4

THE DEADLY DANGER OF MORALISM

"Knowing that a man is not justified by the works of the law but by faith in Jesus Christ, even we have believed in Christ Jesus, that we might be justified by faith in Christ and not by the works of the law; for by the works of the law no flesh shall be justified."

—GALATIANS 2:16

What can Christians do to help halt the spiritual and moral decline in America? Many believe the best solutions are political activism, judicial challenges, public protests, organized boycotts, educational programs, and other kinds of organized civic efforts. By such means they hope to elevate the standard of morality in American society and thereby win God's blessing for our nation.

On a purely human level, the rationale behind that kind of thinking is easy to understand. The courts, the legislature, and even local school boards have participated in systematically undermining the morality of America. The sexual revolution, abortion on demand, and similar changes in public policy have spawned a host of evils that have disfigured American society. No one who truly loves the Lord and believes the Bible can possibly support the policies that drive those trends.

As Christians, we zealously desire goodness, integrity, decency, and morality to be the hallmarks of our society. God's law exalts virtue; His will as revealed in Scripture demands it. Certainly in every way and at every opportunity, we ought to pursue and promote biblical morality. What Christian could do less?

Moreover, as true Christians, we despise every form of evil. What genuine believer doesn't hate the wanton killing of unborn infants? What Christian doesn't oppose pornography, drug abuse, and the promotion of various sexual perversions? In our utter contempt for such things, all Christians ought to be in full agreement.

It is right for us to oppose the sins of our society, and it is right that Christians as individuals should voice our objection in the voting booth and by speaking out in other ways.

MISTAKING THE SYMPTOMS FOR THE DISEASE

But are political movements and moral crusades the ultimate answer to the evils that threaten America? Can the spiritual decline in our nation be reversed through legislation and moral reform alone? Is that where the church should be investing its energies? Can a political coalition of Christians and non-Christians based on shared moral values really work to the benefit of the cause of Christ? Is that what the evangelical movement in America should be pursuing? Is there any mandate in Scripture for the church to try to organize political coalitions and work for moral reform in secular society through social activism? Is the so-called Religious Right the answer to what ails America?

The Deadly Danger of Moralism

The widespread growth of Christian political activism seems to be rooted in the misconception that morality is the answer to everything wrong with society. People think if America becomes moral, God will bless America. They are therefore desperate to put prayer back in classrooms and get the Ten Commandments back on courtroom walls, as if mere icons of biblical faith and the external trappings of Christianity were enough to guarantee God's favor on the nation.

But restoring Christian symbols to public places would be only cosmetic, like makeup on a harlot. Legislation to promote moral reform is too superficial to be a real solution. The moral decline in America is merely the *symptom* of our nation's spiritual malaise, and we dare not confuse the symptom with the disease. The cure for a brain tumor is not aspirin to make the headache go away. Likewise, the cure for America's spiritual ills is not merely reform of some laws and policies. The real solution is one that strikes at the root of the problem. It is a solution that answers the problem of sin. It is the way of salvation set forth in the gospel.

To be perfectly clear: Morality and even religion per se will not invite or secure the blessing of God. Morality and religion alone will not gain our nation an ounce of divine favor. America could be *both* more moral and more religious, and yet not escape divine judgment. The influence of Pharisaism in Jesus' time did not avert the devastating judgment of God in A.D. 70, when the entire city of Jerusalem was laid waste by godless Romans. Jesus Himself had warned on several occasions that the external morality being propagated by the Pharisees was not sufficient to save individuals from judgment, and not sufficient to save the nation from impending destruction. In other words, He rejected the "Religious Right" of His own era and promised judgment. The most stringent and exacting morality was no defense. In fact, it was an offense to God because they used their morality as a mask behind which to hide their rejection of His Son.

God blesses only one thing: saving faith in His Son, the Lord Jesus Christ. "But without faith it is impossible to please Him" (Hebrews 11:6). Scripture teaches this repeatedly: "Those who are in the flesh *cannot please God*. But you are not in the flesh but in the Spirit, if indeed the Spirit of God dwells in you. Now if anyone does not have the Spirit of Christ, he is not His" (Romans 8:8–9). Anyone who does not believe in and love the Lord Jesus Christ is among the cursed. John 3:18 says, "He who believes in Him is not condemned; but he who does not believe is condemned already, because he has not believed in the name of the only begotten Son of God." Clearly, union with Christ by faith is the one way to avert ultimate judgment: "He who believes in the Son has everlasting life; and he who does not believe the Son shall not see life, but the wrath of God abides on him" (v. 36). "If anyone does not love the Lord Jesus Christ, let him be accursed" (1 Corinthians 16:22).

WHY HUMAN "GOODNESS" WON'T SOLVE OUR NATION'S PROBLEMS

As Christians, of course we support morality. We're certainly not in favor of *im*morality. I'm not against those who hate evil and wickedness; I am *among* them. There are occasionally some temporal, superficial benefits to be gained by using the democratic process to mitigate public indecency and to oppose immoral policies. I don't oppose such efforts within their proper limits. But they cannot become the church's main strategy for influencing our nation. "For the weapons of our warfare are not carnal but mighty in God for pulling down strongholds, casting down arguments and every high thing that exalts itself against the knowledge of God, bringing every thought into captivity to the obedience of Christ" (2 Corinthians 10:4–5). In other words, we are engaged in a battle for the truth against lies. And the best way to thwart the lies of demons and men is by answering those lies with God's revealed truth. That means our best weapon in this

78

warfare is not the *carnal* political process, but the *mighty* proclamation of God's Word—preaching *the gospel* in particular. Moral reform and legislative efforts that leave people in unbelief are worthless for any eternal good.

We must understand that divine favor can never be earned by human "goodness." The good works of sinful people cannot merit divine favor either individually or collectively, because our best works always fall short of the standard of perfection God demands. God's standard is even higher than the ultra-fastidious legal righteousness the Pharisees exemplified. Jesus said, "For I say to you, that unless your righteousness exceeds the righteousness of the scribes and Pharisees, you will by no means enter the kingdom of heaven" (Matthew 5:20).

The Pharisees' rigid adherence to Moses' law set a standard never even attempted by most people. If *that* wasn't good enough, we have to ask, "How high is God's standard?" Jesus was clear; it is the absolute perfection of God Himself: "Therefore you shall be perfect, just as your Father in heaven is perfect" (v. 48). Any "good works" that fall short of that standard simply cannot earn merit with God. That is why the best of human good works are likened to "filthy rags" in Isaiah 64:6. They are an offense to God—a reason for condemnation, not blessing. The only good works that are worthy of God's blessing are the works of Christ on our behalf—His perfect righteousness imputed to those who believe.

Therefore the remedy for society's immorality cannot be *moralism* (religion reduced to moral practice). Moralism damns just like immorality. Moralism cannot bring divine blessing. That is why Jesus regularly went head to head with the moralistic people in His world. In fact, He reserved His most scathing, searing, severe invectives for them. That ought to be reason enough for the church to be wary of the agenda promoted by the modern Religious Right.

JESUS' PREACHING AGAINST MORALISM

In Matthew 23:13–39, Jesus pronounced a series of woes on the religious leaders of His time. Again, these were the *most* moral people of His society, people who were obsessive about keeping the smallest of Old Testament laws and Jewish traditions. They even gave a tithe of the little seeds in their spice cabinets! (v. 23). Yet Jesus' discourse against them was the harshest sermon He ever gave. He condemned their moralism as mere hypocrisy: "Woe to you, scribes and Pharisees, hypocrites! For you are like whitewashed tombs which indeed appear beautiful outwardly, but inside are full of dead men's bones and all uncleanness. Even so you also outwardly appear righteous to men, but inside you are full of hypocrisy and lawlessness" (vv. 27–28).

Jesus never used harsh words like that against the outcasts, the prostitutes, the tax-collectors, or the criminals of His day. In fact, He spent His time ministering graciously to such people—so much so that the Pharisees accused Him of being "a glutton and a winebibber, a friend of tax collectors and sinners!" (Luke 7:34).

Moralism was never the message of the Old Testament prophets. It was never the message of the

Messiah. It was never the message of the apostles. It is not the message of the New Testament. It has never been God's message to the world. In fact, God's assessment of moralism is given in Isaiah 57:12: "I will declare your righteousness and your works, for *they will not profit you*" (emphasis added).

The apostle Paul characterized his own pre-conversion lifetime of Pharisaical moralism as "rubbish" (Philippians 3:9 NASB). The Greek word he used was very explicit: *skubalon.* It means "dung."

Whatever superficial morality people may exhibit, it earns no merit with God. It gains nothing. "By the deeds of the law no flesh will be justified in His sight" (Romans 3:20).

Degenerate people can sometimes become more moral. The scoundrel turns over a new leaf. Political organizations can sometimes achieve a degree of "moral rearmament" in society. People who have failed miserably can, to some degree, reorder their lives. The delinquent youth can decide to live a better life to impress a girlfriend. But when such changes are nothing but fleshly willpower divorced from faith in Christ, they are ultimately all for naught.

The biblical message is not that humanity is divided between the moral and the immoral. The clear message of the Bible is that "all have sinned and fall short of the glory of God" (Romans 3:23). There is no division between *good* people and *bad* people; all are sinners, and all deserve condemnation. The moral unbeliever may actually be in a *worse* state than the profligate sinner, because the moral person does not understand his own need. Jesus said, "Those who are well have no need of a physician, but those who are sick. I did not come to call the righteous, but sinners, to repentance" (Mark 2:17).

Whatever level of external morality a person might attain, he or she is a condemned sinner apart from Christ. You might be the most moral Pharisee in Israel; you might be the most generous philanthropist in your town; you might be the most clean-living student in the college dorm; you might be the kindest and most active parent in the PTA; or you might be the most devoted follower of the latest spiritual fad. But without Christ, you're going to hell with the dope dealers and prostitutes. Unless you've been reconciled to God through His Son Jesus Christ, all the morality in the world will not help you. "For as many as have sinned without law will also perish without law, and as many as have sinned in the law will be judged by the law" (Romans 2:12). Either way, if you are counting on your own merit to save you, you are doomed.

What's Wrong With Moralism?

Moralism holds a number of deadly dangers. I can think of at least sixteen reasons why Christians should not embrace moralism as a strategy for curing the evils of our society:

1. It is not our commission. Second Corinthians 5:20 describes the proper role of the Christian in society: "Therefore we are ambassadors for Christ, as though God were pleading through us: we implore you on Christ's behalf, be reconciled to God." We are Christ's ambassadors. Although that may sound like a political calling, it is not. We are a kingdom of priests, not politicians. A priest is a reconciler. And that is what we are called to do: to implore people to be reconciled to God.

We are not called to stand apart from society and point fingers; we are called to go into all the world and make disciples (Matthew 28:19–20). When believers become confused about what God has called us to do—when they make moralizing society their top priority—they abandon their true mission. When the church elevates the pursuit of cultural morality above the biblical mandate to proclaim the gospel, it essentially forfeits its distinctive voice and takes its place among a myriad of lobbyist groups and political parties peddling earthly agendas. *Heaven's* agenda is summed up in the Great Commission; it is the task of evangelism, not political and moral reform.

2. It wastes immense amounts of precious resources. When the church invests time, money, and human energy in political causes, we waste our resources. It ultimately matters very little whether someone goes to hell as a prostitute or a policeman. Our energies should not be spent just trying to make sinners better people. We need to be telling them the solution to sin and the way of salvation. All this effort to clean up America smacks of trying to make the leopard change his spots (Jeremiah 13:23). It is a waste of the church's resources.

Ephesians 5:16–17 says, "[Redeem] the time, because the days are evil. Therefore do not be unwise, but understand what the will of the Lord is." The will of the Lord is clear: we are called to preach the message of reconciliation and implore people to be reconciled to God. To do something else is to be foolish and to waste time and resources. We're not interested in making cosmetic changes to our nation's moral climate. We ought to be proclaiming the saving gospel of Jesus

Christ through which God saves people from their sins and gives them new hearts and eternal life.

3. *Moral reform is a frustrating and ultimately impossible task.* Moralism aims at an unattainable goal: the improvement of society without any transformation of people's souls. The leopard *cannot* change his spots. Sinners cannot reform themselves. And therefore society as a whole cannot be truly reformed unless people are made new creatures in Christ (2 Corinthians 5:17).

4. *Moralism misconstrues the nature of God's kingdom.* Those who aim only at moral reform usually misunderstand the kingdom of God. In John 18:36, Jesus said, "My kingdom is not of this world. If My kingdom were of this world, My servants would fight." We're not trying to preserve our nation's status in the world or preserve some earthly culture. To spend all one's time, energy and effort striving for political power and influence misses the point of God's kingdom. Jesus told His disciples, "You know that the rulers of the Gentiles lord it over them, and those who are great exercise authority over them. *Yet it shall not be so among you*" (Matthew 20:25–26, emphasis added). The quest for earthly political influence is incompatible with the purposes of God's kingdom.

Furthermore, the prosperity of the kingdom of God in no way rises or falls with political fortunes in America. The ultimate advancement of God's kingdom will not be thwarted by any kind of politics or immorality in America or anywhere else.

5. *Moralism asks sinners to do what only God can do.* You and I cannot make other people more moral. They cannot reform themselves enough to make any eternal difference, either. A bad tree cannot bear good fruit (Matthew 7:18). We cannot even discern our own hearts, much less make them pure (Jeremiah 17:9). The transformation of a human soul is God's work and God's alone. And He accomplishes this work through the instrumentality of His Word (1 Peter 1:23).

6. *Moralism is a religion devoid of theology.* For the most part, the Religious Right in America has nothing to do with theology. That is by design. The Religious Right is a coalition of people who share a basic political conservatism but often have little in common theologically. So they avoid dealing with theological issues. Consequently, many people in the movement are ignorant of sound doctrine, ignorant of the Scriptures, and even ignorant of the true God. They are trying to accomplish something that has no theological underpinnings.

I'm very concerned about efforts at morality that are not undergirded with sound theology and driven by a concern for the glory of God. Such efforts are doomed from the start, because they don't have either the right motive or the right goal.

7. Moralism misconstrues what it means to be salt and light. In Matthew 5:13–14, Jesus said to His disciples, "You are the salt of the earth . . . You are the light of the world." Ironically, those statements are often quoted as a justification for political activism. But salt and light are not symbols of our moral influence or political power; those figures represent the gospel witness and the power of holy living. That is how Jesus used the imagery in His Sermon on the Mount. Light represents the shining forth of truth. Salt is the preservative power of godly living. As light, we proclaim the truth; as salt we add seasoning and act as a preservative in society by manifesting righteous works in our own lives. Being salt and light has nothing to do with any political strategy.

8. Moralism has no New Testament model except the Pharisees. All the Pharisees' efforts to moralize people were counterproductive. Jesus said, "Woe to you, scribes and Pharisees, hypocrites! For you travel land and sea to win one proselyte, and when he is won, you make him twice as much a son of hell as yourselves" (Matthew 23:15).

Furthermore, there is no New Testament model for political action. Jesus didn't try to overthrow slavery. The apostles didn't organize protests against the immorality, inequity, abusive tax system, or even the ruthless persecution of Christians by the Roman Empire. Nothing in Scripture suggests we are called to such a task.

9. Political efforts to moralize society result in unholy unions with unbelievers and enemies of the gospel. Lots of unbelievers, members of religious cults, and people from religious traditions that skew or reject the gospel nonetheless favor moral reform. Evangelicals have formed political coalitions with such people. But what happens? In order to keep the coalition together, you have to eliminate the preaching of the gospel. When we are aligned politically with people who are offended by the gospel, our testimony is hindered and our ability to minister effectively is hamstrung. It is a serious mistake to forge such alliances (2 Corinthians 6:14–17).

10. Moralism leads to inclusivism and works-salvation. Political coalition-building starts to eat away people's convictions about the exclusivity of Christ. This trend is very evident among American evangelicals at the moment. Many now say they believe heaven will include people from non-Christian faiths—perhaps even some agnostics with high moral standards. They have redefined the way of salvation in moralistic terms and rendered the gospel moot. In effect, faith has been deposed by human works in their theology.

11. *Moralism is selective about the sins it attacks.* One doesn't hear the Religious Right arguing with much enthusiasm against pride or materialism. I haven't seen them mounting any great campaign against divorce. They rarely even decry the sin of adultery. They are vocal against sins like homosexuality, pedophilia, abortion, pornography, and other shocking or perverted forms of sin.

But they don't even deal with the worst sin of all. What's that? Consider this: If the first and Great Commandment is Matthew 22:37, "You shall love the LORD your God with all your heart, with all your soul, and with all your mind," then the greatest sin would be any violation of that commandment. You want to talk about morality? Let's talk about *that*. You want to talk about sin? Let's not pick out five we can most easily assault because we don't do those sins. Let's talk about the greatest of all commandments. Why is that not part of the agenda of the Religious Right? If we are going to go after America's immorality, then let's indict people (including ourselves) where we need to be indicted most—for not loving God as we ought to.

12. *Moralism fails to understand the true nature of spiritual warfare.* Many in the American Religious Right are convinced they are waging warfare in the spiritual arena. But this is not the kind of warfare to which Scripture calls us. Again, true spiritual warfare is described in 2 Corinthians 10:4–5. It entails smashing down erroneous ideologies with the truth of God's Word, "bringing every thought into captivity to the obedience of Christ." This battle is not waged against flesh-and-blood enemies, and it is not advanced by political strategies that are nothing more than worldly wisdom. It is certainly not the kind of battle currently being waged by the Religious Right in America.

13. *The politics of moralism makes those we are supposed to reach with the gospel into enemies.*

Unbelievers, immoral people, pornographers, homosexuals, and abortionists have become vilified and hated among believers. We tend to regard them as our enemies. But they are our mission field. We mustn't become like Jonah, who hated the Ninevites so much that he would do anything to avoid preaching to them. And even after they responded to his preaching and a revival swept that city, Jonah sulked, because he wanted God to destroy all those people!

The Ninevites were indeed wretched people. They slaughtered their enemies and built pyramids out of the skulls of their victims. They loved torture and bloodshed and violence. In terms of earthly measurements of wickedness, they were far worse sinners than the enemies of today's Religious Right. But God displayed his love and mercy to them, and he rebuked Jonah for not having compassion toward them.

There is a legitimate holy hatred of sin. But Jesus wept with compassion over sinners. So must we.

14. *The politics of moralism brings persecution*

and hatred of Christians for the wrong reasons. It is a privilege and honor to suffer reproach for the sake of Christ (Matthew 5:11). But people who call themselves Christians today are being vilified by the world for their political positions and for their hostility toward the very people we are supposed to be trying to reach. That actually hurts the testimony of the church.

15. *Moralism reverses the divine order.* Moralism makes morality the power for salvation, rather than vice versa. Many evangelicals today seem to operate with the notion that if we can elevate the morality of our culture, then more people will believe the gospel. They imagine that if we can clean up the country, it will afford greater opportunities for the gospel. That's exactly the reverse of the divine order.

16. *Moralism fails to understand the wrath of God.* We saw in chapter 3 how God often abandons people to their sin because of His wrath. Do we imagine that moral reform and political machinations can overturn the wrath of God? We don't know what God's plan for America is, but we do know the mandate He has given to the church, and that mandate has to do with proclaiming the gospel, and that alone.

Moralism confuses and misses the priority for what Christians ought to be doing in the world. It misrepresents the divine message that all people, moral or immoral, are damned and must be saved. And they can be saved only by believing the gospel.

Remember this: It is people who consider themselves highly moral and deeply religious who are trying to kill Americans by flying airplanes into our buildings. For that matter, it was people who thought of themselves as highly moral and deeply religious who conspired with the Romans to crucify Christ. The moral and the immoral schemed together to kill Him, and in His dying He provided the salvation they both desperately needed.

Moralism isn't the answer to what ails America. The gospel is. Higher moral standards alone won't earn God's blessing on this country. Our only hope for that lies in the transforming power of the gospel. And our calling is to preach the gospel of Jesus Christ to the ends of the earth, regardless of what unbelievers in our nation do. May God give His people grace to be faithful to that task. I believe it is the most significant blessing He could ever bestow on this nation.

ENDNOTES

CHAPTER THREE

1. *The Ann Landers Encyclopedia* (New York: Doubleday, 1978), 514–17.
2. Wayne W. Dyer, *Your Erroneous Zones* (New York: Funk & Wagnalls, 1976), 90–91.